Iced Tea Poetry

"You can find poetry in your everyday life,
your memory, in what people say on the bus,
in the news, or just what's in your heart."

~ Carol Ann Duffy

Also by Greg Stidham:

Blessings and Sudden Intimacies (PathBinder Publishers, 2021)

Dear Friends, (PathBinder Publishers, 2021)

Doctoring in Nicaragua (Finishing Line Press, 2021)

Iced Tea Poetry

ICED TEA POETRY

by

Greg Stidham

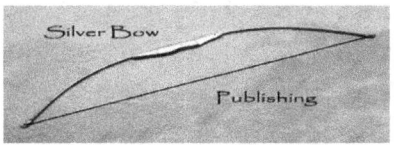

720 Sixth Street, Box # 5
New Westminster, BC
CANADA V3L 3C5

Title: Iced Tea Poetry
Author: Greg Stidham
Cover Art: "Surreal Pastel Tulips" painting by Candice James
Layout and Editing: Candice James
ISBN: 9781774032671(print)
ISBN: 9781774032688 (e-book)

All rights reserved including the right to reproduce or translate this book or any portions thereof, in any form except for the use of short passages for review purposes, no part of this book may be reproduced, in part or in whole, or transmitted in any form or by any means, electronically or mechanically, including photocopying, recording, or any information or storage retrieval system without prior permission in writing from the publisher or a license from the Canadian Copyright Collective Agency (Access Copyright)

ISBN: 9781774032671 Print
ISBN: 9781774032688 eBook
© 2023 Silver Bow Publishing

Library and Archives Canada Cataloguing in Publication

Title: Iced tea poetry / by Greg Stidham.
Names: Stidham, Greg, author.
Identifiers: Canadiana (print) 20230464254 | Canadiana (ebook) 20230464297 | ISBN 9781774032671
   (softcover) | ISBN 9781774032688 (Kindle)
Classification: LCC PS8637.T535 I24 2023 | DDC

Iced Tea Poetry

I thank my wife, Pam,
for her enduring patience and support.

I would also like to thank poet Jesse Graves
for invaluable editorial assistance and suggestions.

Iced Tea Poetry

CONTENTS

Living

Early Shift at Walmart / 13
The Possum / 14
The Birds Know / 15
The Bells of Idlewild / 16
Spring Equinox / 17
Raccoon Hour / 18
Evolution / 19
Passing Stroller in Early Evening / 20
Abandoned Farmhouse / 21
Afternoon Walk / 22
Girl in the Airport / 23
Passing the Amish in Upstate New York / 24
Autumn Surprise / 25

Elegies

Death Bed / 29
Clementines / 30
Vision / 31
The Vigil / 32
My Father's Sweater / 33
Debbie / 34

Foibles

Boxes / 37
Family Gathering / 38
New Epileptic / 39
Surgery / 40
Icy Deck / 41
Old Man / 42

Doubt / 43
Ballroom Dancing / 44

Best Friends

P.D. / 47
Best Friend / 48
Smokey / 49
Time / 50
Dexter Loves the Snow / 51
Huntress / 52
Minnie's Going Deaf / 53
Canine Emotions / 54
An Elegy / 55

Bees and Other Creatures

Bumblebee / 59
Abandoned Hive / 60
Worker Bees / 61
Lying with Honeybees / 62
Early Blossoms / 63
Canadian Geese / 64
Mayflies / 65

Places

KOA / 69
Getting dressed after showering at a KOA / 70
Ontario Thaw / 71
Ontario Spring 72
Nebraska Breeze at Sunset / 73
Sandhill Cranes / 74
Windmills in the High Plains / 75
Sweet-Scented Storm / 76
Easter / 77

Mississippi August / 78
So This is Memphis / 79
Noodling the Wolf River / 81
Cicada Symphony / 82
Mississippi Delta / 83
Ontario December / 84
Late Ontario Snow / 85
Morning Red Fox / 86

Medicine and Grieving

Anatomy Lab / 89
Off to Work / 90
Taxis in Managua / 91
Doctoring in Nicaragua / 92
Central Market, Managua / 93
Imagine / 94
The Lock / 95
Bad News / 96
Powerless / 97
Delivery 98
Crossing the Plains / 99
Holding a Baby / 101
Parent Support Group / 102

Contrition

Finality / 105
Twentieth Anniversary / 106
Twenty-First Anniversary / 107
New Year's Eve / 108

Creation

Late Night Visitor / 111
Inspiration / 112

Farewell to Literal Poems / 113
Pens and Indentations / 114
The Importance of a Rabbit / 115
Iced Tea Poetry / 116

Acknowledgements / 117

Iced Tea Poetry

Living

Iced Tea Poetry

Early Shift at Walmart

Descending blue-breasted on the back doors
an hour before opening time,
they are like water-birds descending
together onto slow-moving bayou waters.

Leather-faced, long pure-white shocks
and smile hints of youthful handsomeness,
one readies to shopping-cart greet you
while the middle-aged Latina
with two missing teeth unlocks and replaces
an empty drawer with another bill-filled.

And Keisha, eggplant-colored hair
above the six-ring pierced left lobe
and tiny eyebrow bead, puts in order
cases of cosmetics, tubes
of lip-color, and vials of ersatz scents
mimicking expensive ones,
her short skirt teasing as she
reaches to replace top-shelf items.

Here are stories and memories and
lives... newborn babies,
breast cancer mastectomies,
parents incarcerated with Alzheimer's,
lust bubbling up like lava,
God's microcosm of his creation.

The Possum
       (after Ted Kooser)

I read a poem about an opossum
today that touched me,
and reminded me of a possum
in the garage of my wife's former house.

Like the possum in the poem,
she was pink. She looked at us, calm,
her pink tongue poised at her pointed lips,
her pink fingers raised as if in prayer.
She wasn't afraid, she didn't flee.
She didn't attack in a frenzy of sharp claws.
She sat and looked at us
as though awaiting
a fate she could not know.

She let us guide her
into a screened cage box covered
with a blanket to keep it dark,
and keep her calm.

We fed her niblets of dog food,
kept a water dish full until next night;
in the dark, we moved the cage
to the back yard, lifted the screen gate
and waited, while she waited to see
if we were serious about her freedom.
Next morning, the cage was empty.

The Birds Know

The birds know,
two days in a row,
singing spring songs.

Banks of snow three
feet tall make walking
shoveled sidewalks like

crouching through bunkers,
or tripping through maze hedgerows.

Sun beams back from
blank whiteness everywhere,
and breath still frosts like pure exhaust.

But the birds know:
March begins tomorrow.

The Bells of Idlewild

The clamor of a hundred bells,
at first a thunderous cacophony
at noon, until layers of sound
are quietly peeled away.

At last a single sonorous bell
tolls once, twice, three
times slowly before
fading into the bell tower
silhouetted by afternoon sun.

Spring Equinox

Today and tonight are equal,
one of two times this year.
The first day of spring
brings freeze tonight,
and my bees didn't survive,
drowned in their own beauty
and their own humidity, because
I failed them, forgot to install
the upper entrance,
essential for ventilation.

As a child I forgot to change
water in my goldfish bowl.
I cried in bed that night.

Raccoon Hour

Half past one and
more than half past
a six-pack of artisanal beer,
heady father-son conversation
about civil rights and doctoring,
politics, and whether parents
should take their kids to church.

A crash of metal in the backyard black
brings out searching flashlights,
spotlighting the empty yard,
and then the two
silver stars stare back,
quiet, quivering nervously.

Evolution

The creek on red clay was little more
than a drainage ditch behind construction,
houses in a new subdivision.

As a boy I looked down into the several
inches of clear water, like a terrible God,
or Godzilla filling the sky of the tadpoles,
who darted in frantic fear stirring
tiny trails of silt dust.

Silver fish slivers now, in a month
they'll sprout little leg buds.
Then soon they will reproduce
the entire first half of evolution.

Passing Stroller in Early Evening

Straw boater perched atop his likely balding pate,
John Lennon-like lenses straddling his nose,
he followed the high-tech silver stroller,
spoked wheels smooth and silent.

He chattered endlessly to the chubby
bare-footed legs kicking out in front,
all that I could see of a happy child.

Abandoned Farmhouse

The 1850's farmhouse hid
deep in the pine woods behind
post-war split levels, beneath
a canopy of branches that made dusk
of mid-day.

It leaned askew like
an arthritic octogenarian
on the handle of his cane,
the wood of the walls coal gray
and splintered, gap-toothed
like the witch we imagined once lived there,
my best friend and I.

We were sure no one else
knew of the house we now
claimed as ours, our hideout.
The wood flooring not yet rotted through
was covered with brittle yellow newspaper,
and no sign of recent life except
a nest of leaves and paper scraps,
and a few unrolled condoms
whose purpose we could not yet guess.

Afternoon Walk

Shaky hands-on shiny metal
handlebars, big-spoked wheels
turning slow, like a fan
with power turned down,
he pushed her from behind.

He stopped to fix the footrests
to hold her flaccid legs more comfortably,
while the hot afternoon sun reflected
from his brushed-back silver hair,
before they resumed their afternoon walk
around the neighborhood block.

Girl in the Airport

Moist eyes gaze past
fast food kiosks,
past milling children flying
paper airplanes, playing
paper-scissors-rock,
her ears deaf
to the din that drives
most to distraction.
Her nose
is slightly rosy
and her eyes
she blots with a napkin,
and like a lab
emerging from a lake
she tosses her head
to shake off sadness like water.

Passing the Amish in Upstate New York

Driving up Highway 12 in Jefferson County,
up toward the banks of the St. Lawrence,
the black buggy came into view, topping a gentle hill,
the trees with their last late-autumn leaves
still clinging to their colors and their branches,
winding through curves and over hills,
the sky brilliant blue, sun shining brightly,
belying the near-freezing temperatures outside.

The bearded man with his full-brimmed black hat,
reins in one hand, crop in the other,
called to the elegant stallion at full canter.
His wife beside him, thick shawl-wrapped
like a mummy, scarf around her neck
and head and bonnet atop,
hugged herself against the cold.

Seeing their faces passing I waved impulsively,
and she nodded, too wise to the cold
to unwrap an arm to wave.

Autumn Surprise

A September sunflower pokes its corona up
surprising through tired soil
while other summer blooms droop,
presaging the coming of winter hibernation.

Soon this ground
will be buried in white,
the cold turning breath
into mist clouds.

But somehow surviving the onslaught of
scavenging squirrels hoarding for winter,
this yellow splash of optimism is startling,
like the sun suddenly blinding
from between dark clouds
at the end of a tornadic thunderstorm.

Iced Tea Poetry

Elegies

Death Bed
(for Kent)

Your thin white hair balanced
the thin-trimmed moustache
as you lay, head propped,
bathed in calmness,
welcoming two visitors
with a frail half-hug.

Your death bed was the same bed
you'd slept in for twenty years,
the one you and Cathy made love in,
more carefully with the passing years,
the same one where you lay
in the warm smells of each other,
hints of lavender lotion and Old Spice,
chatting into wee hours,
or holding hands at the end of a day
of finishing finally your last book,
the one you wouldn't see in print.

Clementines
      (for Gerry)

I pulled a ripe clementine
from my parka's pocket and handed it
to my friend whose eyes widened.
He sat up in his bed and took
the orange orb into a shaky hand.
Using his thumbnail he dug out
the divot at the fruit's north pole,
then stripped the skin down
like peeling old wallpaper.

Once the orange
was naked of its skin
he broke off two wedges,
slipped them between his lips.

"After chemo my taste buds die,
you know, and in a week or so,
when the stem cells take,
my taste returns."

He took another wedge in his mouth,
tossed the scraps of skin
in the waste basket by his bed,
adjusted the arm with the IV
and lay back, eyes resting closed,
faint smile on his parched cracked lips.

Vision
    (for John)

The world peers in on him, spying
through a milky crystal of gypsum,
the same through which he peers out.

He still sees, but more now
with hands and fingers, as he tends
the tendrils of bean sprouts in the back garden
of his hundred-year-old Ohio River house.

His wife touches lightly on his elbow
as they make their way up
the concrete front steps.

The Vigil
     (for my mother)

Beside your bed I sit and listen
to the not-quite snore of coma-breathing
and wipe the dried trickle of saliva
from your lip and cheek.

They said to talk to you:
"You never know what they hear."
But what chat can there be
while we await your death,

and you hold on, don't let go
for forever, for whatever
reason none of us know,
and all I can think of is

your bones riddled with
kidney cells gone mad, and
locked tight in my memory
you'll never know you'd snored,
never know you'd drooled.

My Father's Sweater

Dark December night
made cold by frugal thermostating,
and lost and longing moved-out wife—
too quiet and lonely for a fire,
even one suffused with a cabernet.

And I wander from office
to bedroom, bedroom to living room,
and then upstairs closet,
seeking thrifty warmth.

I put my arms
into baggy sleeves
of my father's sweater
that my mother
knit, or crocheted.

I always thought it so staid,
so boring, so embarrassing,
but still it ended up
in my upstairs closet,
long after they were gone.

Debbie
(Deborah Jean Stidham,
1953-1954)

Sixty-five years on now lying
under a few feet of well-groomed
central Ohio sod, in a box not much larger
than an ornate shoebox.

Six months she never lived at home,
but in a home with other infants like her:
Lucite bassinets lined up in rows, each with its
swaddling blanket, feeding tube hanging from above.

Tagging along at three I followed
hand-held while my parents went to visit,
and through the bay window
on the porch where I waited,

I'd see not my sister or my parents,
but all the other sick babies.

Foibles

Iced Tea Poetry

Boxes
       (for Chris)

One more box and
one too many memories,
this packing a month ago
and unpacking now
in a new place, I've
stumbled upon photos of
my second-grade son,
his curly-haired cohorts,
and his two teachers
with their bob-cuts
and lipstick and
just-for-photo smiles.

His immunization records,
no use anymore,
and the report card signed
once by mom and seven times by dad,
and finally the memory
of that first day of school,
the brown bag lunch
so carefully assembled
and healthfully planned.

He was so stoic, and I thought
only I had pangs in the chest,
the sting in the eyes,
until the confession twenty years later,
that he was scared to death.

Family Gathering

The chains holding the wooden swing
squeak softly while the old man's legs
sway the bench gently to and fro,
and the late-afternoon sun breaks through
the few gaps in the leafed-out front yard trees.

A minivan has drawn up, flooding out
a tsunami of kids who jump and scream
"Grandpa!" and hug the two dogs.
The two women begin to chat,
the dad plays ball with his son.

This Norman Rockwell scene is over
in fifteen minutes. They pour back into the van
like gravy on Thanksgiving turkey and honking,
are gone, the son never speaking
to the old man still swinging.

New Epileptic

Stooping now
to retrieve a dropped pen
then standing again,
an act so ordinary
the brief passing
vertigo once
unnoticed now
triggers thoughts
of unruly neurons
plotting their next
choreography
the next slapstick
they'll direct
at my expense,
my pride,
perhaps even
my breath.

Surgery

Strong arms of attendants assist the move,
shimmying butt and torso from gurney
to hard metal table, where I lie
watching the drip of clear fluids
in the plastic chambers of the IV's.

Education made me know
more than what is wise—
the size of the endotracheal tube,
the mammoth instrument in my throat
that makes the tube's insertion possible,
and the remote prospect of missing the target.

I'd heard of anesthesia not working,
immobilized patients feeling
every scalpel cut, unable to cry out.

Watching the familiar white medicine
I hoped would put me to sleep,
dripping in the tubing,

until I awoke, being lifted again,
back onto the gurney,
the blazing white sun
blinding my eyes alive.

Icy Deck

Walking to my car over the backyard deck,
covered with a layer of ice from falling rain
prior to plummeting temperatures,
clear and sparkling as any glass,
my foot slides out with a mind of its own,
my backside landing sore on the first step down,
and I stare up at a black sky dotted
with frost-hidden stars and
contemplate my insignificance.

Old Man

An old man in baggy trousers sits
in dim shadows of an empty cathedral,
watching dust floaters dancing in sunbeams
filtered through kaleidoscopic stained glass.
He doesn't pray, but stares straight ahead,
sniffing the slight scent of old incense.
He doesn't express contrition
nor pray for forgiveness,
but removes from his pocket
a handkerchief and blows his nose.

Doubt

The wind gusts from over Lake Ontario
carrying frozen fog that stings the face
like tiny electric shocks. The walk home
from work along the shore at night in black

is broken only by the silver saucer
of a moon half-hidden by cloud.
The touque pulled low by gloved hands
barely shields the ears from frostbite,

and the scarf pulled tight
around the neck blocks out
only some of the cold
slithering down my parka.

Ballroom Dancing

I was a fifteen-year-old janitor
in a second-rate suburban hospital,
where, banished to the basement,
I learned to mop and polish linoleum floors,
learned the temperament of the buffer
that weighed more than I.
I was a rodeo rider who had to tame
the rotating buffer pad, had to teach it
to trust me and follow my commands.
A gentle tip up on the handle,
a smooth glide to the right;
a whispered nudge down,
and she floats to the left
as though tiptoeing on clouds.
What was once like riding an angry bull
became ballroom dancing, our feet
dusting lightly over the ballroom floor together,
just me and the buffer, gliding in time
to the harmonies of her humming motor.

Best Friends

Iced Tea Poetry

P.D.
(for "PuppyDog")

Puppy-harpooned, my heart, ensnared
fourteen years ago by the pointed barb,
broke today after watching
the four-legged seizures
and the four-legged flaccidity that followed,
the culmination of a year of ebbing strength,
until today, the needle into the leg vein,
the flash of blood and the slow injection,
leaving only pain-free peace, and tears.

Best Friend

That's what they say—
man's best friend, even when
he marks his territory in my garden,
and half my tomato plants
are browned on one side,
and my barefoot walks
through the garden to my single beehive
risk baseball-sized piles squishing
between my toes before I see them.

He is a senior dog now, slow on stairs
at night at bedtime, arthritis I think,
like mine, but his bladder is better,
so much better he lasts the night.

Smokey

In the photos, Smokey was young,
his large ears not quite erect,
yet to be grown into,
and the days of our bond and kinship
rose up through years clouded by pain,
just like he did in my dream two nights ago:

Me joyfully piloting an ultralight
aircraft made of cloth, aluminum rods,
and rope of nylon, and looking down
seeing the young Smokey, not the elderly
seizure-stricken shepherd, but
the young and invincible Smokey,
rising up from the ground,
floating gracefully, passing by.
I noticed a fur-bare patch of red skin
and wondered what was wrong, but
he just floated on past, to an altitude
my meager craft could barely envision.

Time

In one of my years seven of yours pass.
I wonder if the world moves seven times
faster, how that must be
like a Charlie Chaplin film
on fast forward, a blur so quick
you nearly miss the pat on your butt,
the scratch on the loose skin of your neck.

At almost seventy I've lived almost
ten of your lives, all in slow motion,
and I've raised as many of your kin
from puppyhood to old age and
brain tumors, kidney failure and seizures,
been the one to call the vet
to help you rest at long last, your photo
adorning my refrigerator door now.

Dexter Loves the Snow

My new dog Dexter
loves the snow, scales
four-foot snow drifts
like a Sherpa, or leaps into them
like an arctic antelope.
The railing on my backyard deck
reaches to Dexter's neck,
beneath eight hoary inches and
is furrowed by his chomping jaws
as he bites down its edge
like a happy snowplow.

Huntress

The huntress dog, adopted homeless
black pointer, now a 10-year old puppy.
She pulled her hamstring bolting
coyote-like after a terrified rabbit
in sage between the piñons.

But tonight she brought back
from her wanderings in the dry dirt yard
the jawbone of a deer with
half its teeth missing,
dropped it on the kitchen floor,
smiling proudly, looking up for praise.

Minnie's Going Deaf

She is called Minnie because she looked
so much like her bigger, older buddy,
their black with white markings.
He's now gone a year.
At thirteen years, she's almost a century.

Arthritis controlled by drugs,
she still hunts rabbits
with the vigor of a huntress half her age.
But no head-turn to her name,
no ear-twitch to the loud
pursed-lipped wolf whistle.

What's left now: the working out
of human-dog sign language,
so her last days can be
the best they can be.

Canine Emotions

She seems depressed.
Just like she did
when her old buddy passed.
She lies inside a shell, curled
mouth to tail, eyes still watchful
as we move about the outdoor deck.

We retrieve wine bottles and
cheese and crackers while she watches,
missing nothing, white whiskers
goatee-like framing nose and chin.

She's peaceful as she ignores
her own deafness.
She watches out
over the backyard garden
of garlic blooms and
lettuce heads, dill weed,
and she seems content,
as do I.

An Elegy
(for Minnie)

Dexter roams the house, lost
like an elderly person with early
dementia, circling the coffee table,
then pushing through the doggie door
to the back porch deck.
He stands at the steps
staring blankly into the garden's
lush blooms, looking lost, looking
for something, before he comes back
through the flapping door
to resume his nervous pacing.

He knows that his canine partner
of three years is gone,
he watched us bury her in the back,
behind the tall pink and yellow
freckled lilies, next to the beehive.
I pat the couch to tell him it is okay
to jump up and sit beside me,
and he does, carefully lifting himself
one leg at a time, and together we sit,
both staring into the distance.

Iced Tea Poetry

Bees
and
Other Creatures

Bumblebee

A white-haired woman in her fifties
walks past my front-yard wooden bench,
with her daughter, or perhaps grandchild.
Their animated hands converse silently,
excitedly, the girl behind mumbling
to make her sign right.

A furry-jacketed bumble bee touches
the tops of grass blades awaiting mowing,
to her the size of tree tops, she
moving one to the next,
as oblivious to me
as were the woman
and the child.

Abandoned Hive

A routine visit to the honeybee hive
to be sure they were thriving,
foraging pollen and nectar.
Opening the hive and removing frames
we thought would be filled
with teeming hordes of honeybees
busy building new honeycomb,
cleaning waxy bassinets
for new eggs, but no!
No bees, no teeming—
naked frames empty of brood,
no eggs, no larvae,
just blankness, and stillness,
the only life left that
of yellow jacket robbers,
stealing old honey,
and a single wax moth,
picking at the remains
of a post-apocalyptic city,
abandoned and empty.

Worker Bees

They descend in droves
from barely discernible flight patterns
before a slow approach to their landing site,
landing gear extended, their orange or yellow
pouches like saddlebags straddling a bicycle.

Scarcely pausing, they scramble in
to deliver their sweet spoils, and without rest
they are off again, to gather another cargo
of pollen and nectar, never complaining.

Lying with Honeybees

Lying back in fresh long grass,
surrounded by the scent
of fertile, still-moist soil,
and dandelions littered about
like a myriad of small suns.

I watch downy creatures drifting by
in an infinite azure sky,
and I hear the contralto buzz
around my head, as honeybees
busily tend their tasks,
foraging nectar and pollen,
blossom to hive, oblivious
to my quiet breathing beside them.

Early Blossoms

Alone on a mesa, a pink crabapple tree
embraces the wind, its branches reaching up
and out like a menorah, its petite blossoms
a pointillist image, mysteriously scintillating.

Up close, the shimmer buzzes:
honeybees feasting on spring's
first Rocky Mountain pollen.

Canadian Geese

They are nearing the end of another season,
necks outstretched, flying formation,
voices breaking like a pubescent boy
cracking into adolescence,
too early for their navigation devices
to be perfectly calibrated,
they fly over, graceful wings
sweeping air like synchronized
crew rowers in water,
west to east first, then returning.

It is still Indian Summer,
and departure can be delayed,
allowing for more thorough preparation
for an arduous voyage south.

Mayflies

Mayfly clouds
dull the evening sun,
and runners flap on sidewalks
in shorts and tank-tops
for the first time in seven months.
It is spring in southern Ontario,
where the male mayfly swarms
circle in wait of the lone female:
they pounce and copulate midair,
because there's no tomorrow for them.

Places

KOA

Like honeybees drawn to fields of yarrow,
they descend circling in their Airstreams,
pop-up tents, pop star motorhomes,
rounding the perimeter, homing in
on the petals of their campsites.
They come from Indiana,
Ohio and Ontario.

They are retirees who limp
to restrooms on operated knees,
they are six-year-olds
racing bikes or scooters
screaming down paved paths.
A few are honeymooners,
 pulling their blinds closed at dusk.

Getting dressed after showering at a KOA campground

is like going to Mass.
Please rise. Be seated.
Stand now. Now
take your seats.
Except for kneeling (thank God),
(my knees wouldn't last,
not even the metal one).
Be seated, one leg into briefs,
now stand, the other leg.
Please be seated, find your socks.

Clark Kent
could change in mere seconds
from a three-piece suit
into cape-and-tights regalia
in a phone booth cubicle
smaller than this one.
I can't help but marvel.

Ontario Thaw

Before the arrival of spring's equinox
the smallest of the Great Lakes begins its thaw.
The melt begins in the middle,
where snow once undulated
like sand raked in a Zen rock garden,
the ice so thick it bore the weight of snowmobiles.
Now the white turns to dark green-gray,
and only along the shore does ice still cling white.
Then, at once, overnight,
the water has waves once more.

Beside the nearby highway
the face of the granite escarpment,
furrowed like an elder's face,
weeps a steady stream of tears
from foot-long icicles.

Ontario Spring

In Ontario in June the kayaks appear
perched on cartops in droves,
like the children in schoolyard playgrounds,
where stickball replaces hockey.
Grandfathers rummage
through deep closets retrieving
fishing rods and reels.
But before June, in May,
straw-hatted and gloved women
wearing short sleeves appear outdoors
in pants below the knees, small shovels in hand,
to begin the tedious tilling of the gardens
in time for the bees' awakening.

Nebraska Breeze at Sunset

The breeze that cools the campsite
bringing relief to a day in the 90s,
has touched many vistas:
fields of soy beans, beaded tassels
atop wheat stalks not yet golden,

and steel-fenced enclosures
crowded with cattle awaiting slaughter,
the stench of manure and death,

and now this: transient air whispers
sweetly over this picnic table,
where I sit easy, reading poetry,
as the breeze saunters in,
bearing the surprise of coolness.

Sandhill Cranes

Endless Nebraska cornfields
still sleeping off winter,
covered with six-inch sepia stubble
and thousands of sandhill cranes
foraging last harvest's leftovers.
It is the half-way point
from Biloxi to Banff,
where they feed
and fatten in the fields,
sleep and meet their mates
on the sandbars and banks
of the Platte River,
the pairs inseparable until death.

Windmills in the High Plains

The wind's reedy oboe
outside the camper trailer,
in a Flying-J lot outside Limon,
where the mountains have faded
into the blue-gray horizon behind,
and rolling land of the high plains
stretches ahead.

On the Eastern horizon,
sticking straight up, tiny toothpicks
in the haze of predawn light.

Then four blades
thin as honeybee legs,
like delicate propellers
of a balsa wood airplane model,
assembled with care,
to be launched airward after
endlessly winding the rubber band,
blades tugging the craft
thirty feet into the sky.

Sweet-Scented Storm

Ozone drifts in the center of a storm.
Lightning erupts white
in weeping windows,
and rain raps in jazzy triplets
on our fiberglass roof.
The camper rocks side to side
like a boat in a storm,
just like this storm.

Easter

This is the darkest night of the year,
it is Holy Saturday, and its hours are
buried in darkness, the skies
above the Rockies starless, overcast.

The only sound is the ghostly howl
of western wind crossing the mesa,
circling through gaps in the logs,
like a forlorn oboe.

In a few hours
the curtain of clouds
will part and the sun rise,
the cold earth
slowly warming again.

Mississippi August

Kudzu-choked pines line
Mississippi highways, while
cotton plants droop
for lack of water these scorched
late August afternoons. And
a surprise wee-hour cloudburst
only whets the thirst
of crops' roots dying dry.
Farmers feel a frenzy from
needed dollars being baked
from their soil, their hardened souls
asking one more time, why?

So This Is Memphis

The heat so hot—
an oven opened
while looking in too closely,
the humidity a sauna towel
wrapping your face, your
torso as you leave your
air-conditioned office.

The evening barely tolerable
despite the porch's ceiling fan,
the mosquitos intelligent,
intent on baiting you into a battle
you cannot possibly win,

while the cicada's symphonic squawks
undulate in the still evening air,
still hot and humid,
fan notwithstanding.

On Beale Street past dusk
the lights turn colorful,
flashing not neon, but nearly,
as visitors stroll past juke joints
turned tourist bars
no true bluesman can afford,
while on the street preteen black kids
tap dance or break dance,
traversing the block in back flips
faster than the tourists can walk.

Beale Street meanders down
to the river front, where
black men loaded paddle-powered riverboats,
hauling bales of cotton up-plank,
soon headed north for lucrative sale.

Iced Tea Poetry

They sweat in heat like their homeland's,
but under the threat of the crack of a whip,
the cotton headed north for money
and for the pristine shirts
of wealthy whites.

Noodling the Wolf River

Just upstream from where the Wolf River
slides its clear water into the Mississippi's mud,
redneck boys probe the banks
with six-foot poles.
July sun broils their bare backs,
water slowly swirling to the belt loops
of their denim cutoffs.
Three of them, young,
blond hair long, with wisps of chin fuzz,
pecs rippling as they prod and poke
in search of bank holes, the small caves
where catfish lay their eggs and lie in wait.

"I got something," one yells, stooping,
reaching under water to his chin,
and like a lifter in a weight room
he grunts up from his squat,
water now a fury, his arm
thrust to the elbow in the mouth
of a forty-pound flathead,
his fingers curled out tight
around the fish's gasping gill.

Cicada Symphony

The cicadas' symphony,
crescendo-decrescendo,
stirs the evening dusk
with the ebb and flow
of an insect concert.

The crusty carcasses
cling to the tree bark long
after death, like skeletons
in suburban yard corners
greeting juvenile trick-or-treaters.

Where do they go, these
falsetto-blessed baritones,
and their basso-embellished backups?
Where do they go when they leave
their perfect bodies still,
still clinging to the sides
of southern oaks in Memphis?

Mississippi Delta

Endless expanses of fields of cotton, rice and soy,
stretch from the river to the horizon
where the crops touch the blaze of the setting sun.
It is said the delta meanders from the lobby
of the Peabody hotel in Memphis,
to Catfish Row in Vicksburg,
the rich black soil giving off its river smell,
guitar picking instead of cotton picking,
the voices of the blues still seeping out through the walls
of juke joints in Clarksdale, Batesville and Helena,
the blues born here a century ago,
where the fields flooded every spring,
and white-hooded cross-burning lynchers roamed
until just decades ago: this land remains alive
as the catfish wallowing in the river's mud.

Ontario December

is a fickle month
with traits of
   multiple personality disorder
temperatures above freezing
a night with patter
   of raindrops on shingles
next morning
   all is encased in ice
   diamond-like glistening
the walkway like an old boardwalk
   wood rotting buckling
   below the foot
ice crust giving way
into the soft snow below

next month the lake
   will be frozen
ice two feet thick
rippled with miniature glaciers
       whose interiors reflect sunlight
   in eerie shades
   of otherworldly aquamarine

Late Ontario Snow

In the beginning
the blanket was pristine,
virginal, a light powder,
twelve inches deep
after a slow descent
from heaven.

Now, stained by salt and sand
and automobile excrement,
it is pushed to the side—
charcoal slush.

Morning Red Fox

Overcast gray Colorado mountain morning,
five inches of snow, dead grass stems
sticking straight up.
14,000-foot Shavano backdrops in the distance,
and then, the red fox stalks, one foot,
one small step at a time, eyes fixed ahead.
Then the bolting blur of a jackrabbit
streaks straight toward the log cabin,
fox springing into lightspeed chase,
till the rabbit finds the firewood pile
and vanishes, while the fox slows
before the wood, stopping,
looking side to side, sniffing.

Finding nothing, he wanders hungrily off,
pausing by a tree to hike a leg,
and disappears,
the rabbit safe once more,
in the connected caverns
within the woodpile.

Medicine and Grief

Iced Tea Poetry

Anatomy Lab

I can see them—medical students
in fifteen years, four-strong,
gathered scalpel-handed around me
about to see first-hand my many foibles.

I wonder what they'll think
of the adipose apron
I swore I'd never have.

Which will discover delighted
the detached half biceps
that made me, flexing,
look like Popeye the Sailorman,
after spinach?

Maybe they will find the reason
my shoulder is so sore
it wakes me at night and makes me
a right-sided-only sleeper.

And the MS plaques I have seen on MRI,
they will see first-hand,
denied even to me up-close-and-personal.
They'll touch and slide their fingers
along the slickness and

will they wonder if these glistening
white sheets made me think differently,
or less well, or love less,
or dream better, I wonder
will they wonder anything at all?

Off to Work
       (Nicaragua, 1996)

The midi-bus hurtles through
pot-holed streets in Managua,
hurrying whites in scrubs
with backpacks between their knees.
The traffic deafens, horns
blaring briefly at every turn:
it's a different language.

The bus's windows are
smoky film frames from fifty years ago,
and images flash by for a quick instant—
children in fresh school uniforms,
blue trousers or skirts, and white shirts;
a rickety wooden cart pulled
by a beleaguered geriatric horse;
a three-car intersection-blocking
accident and an arthritic black-and-white
mini-car with flashing blue lights,
a uniformed coffee-skinned man
directing traffic.

Then suddenly the unmanned
guard house guarding
the parking lot of the children's hospital,
and another endless day begins.

Taxis in Managua

We braved the frantic traffic
of tiny cars, half the size
of cars back home, our lives
in the hands of a taxi driver
whose language we did not share.

The endlessly honking horns
unnerving at first to our ears.
Potholes the size of bomb craters
seemed to tear out the taxi belly,
but she jigged and flitted on.

On the roadside a wooden wagon
pulled by an emaciated horse
whipped viciously by a driver
standing above the two wheels
against the background of a billboard
with the polished picture
of a well-dressed woman feeding paper
into a state-of-the-art Xerox machine.

Doctoring in Nicaragua

Like an old-time silent movie
my memories of Managua flicker
in faded black and white
halting and jerking, just
like the tiny taxis darting
round the roundabouts
punctuating the city's boulevards.

Nurses in starchy white uniforms,
housekeepers with mops at attention,
black-haired children with zippered chests,
healing hearts beating beneath bandages
with the new-found certainty of a metronome.

Central Market, Managua

Squalor spread on three sides.
Ahead, booths aplenty
filled with geriatric fruits,
others with fusty meats
hanging from splintered rafters—
chickens and pigs.

Poor people hawk their goods:
toothpaste and fake leather belts,
hammocks and wood carvings.

The women
beating dough with bare fists
making tortillas on hot
table-sized skillet surfaces,
all in rhythm,
like hearing prayers
while attending Mass.

Imagine
(for the many lost children)

Imagine the unimaginable.
Imagine Neil Armstrong leaping
thirty feet above lunar dust,
proclaiming the first small step for man.

Imagine 40 days of torrential monsoon
observed from the deck of a wooden ship
packed tight with pairs of wild animals,
imagine

the pounding on the door in 1939, the
thunder of bootfall in the black night,
your night-dressed father hustled away.

Imagine your father and your mother
digging their graves at Choeung Ek,

or you, running before your
napalm-slathered burning sister,
imagine.

But imagine fishing
the limp blue body
of your two-year old
only son from the swimming pool
of your best friend, lifeless.

Or holding your newborn infant,
congenital heart disease, at the end,
watching the ventilator turned off,
and hearing the monitor beeps
slow to silence.

Imagine,
        imagine.

The Lock

In the dim room with curtained glass walls,
monitors dark and quiet, I watched him.
With tiny manicure scissors,
the type used to trim a baby's nails,
he snipped a strand of hair
from the very back of the boy's still head—
a near-perfect blond ringlet
he gently slid into a zip-lock baggie.
Pausing, he placed the lock
in the outer pocket of his duffle bag,
likely stuffed with clean and dirty socks,
and underwear from three bedside days
and endless nights sleeping stiffly
in an overstuffed chair.
He kissed the boy's forehead,
stood, and turned,
nodded to me
and walked out the door.

Bad News

The weary man in the white coat
leaned through double doors leading
away from white brightness
and beeps of heartbeats,
into the dim hallway, then
the waiting room, his arms
clasped to his chest clutching
the scorching pain
he would too soon
have to share.

Powerless

The woman with short hair looks
up, finds your eyes, begs
with her salty gaze,
"Please help, do something."

You've already told her
nothing more can be done.
She looks away,
takes her boy's hand in hers,
presses it to her forehead,
her shoulders bobbing like a buoy
in a Newfoundland harbor.
And you are enshrouded
with the darkness of impotence.

Delivery

The package landed on my doorstep.
Eleven in the morning and I was still
in my robe, still sipping strong coffee,
writing thoughts
in a spiral-bound dictation notebook.

A high-end fountain pen seeped ink
in beautifully symmetric lines
no one would notice but me.
They were thoughts of birds,
chickadees hopping about
like chipmunks, they were thoughts
of flying in experimental ultralights,

and thoughts of parents
in agony after losing a child.
Gathered with them last night,
my chest burned with pain
that wasn't quite my own.

Crossing the Plains

The expansive space
of Kansas fields
seen through dirty windows
of a highway-hurtling car,
grass and dirt on the shoulder
a blur that causes the eyes
to stutter in nystagmus.

But farther, out by the horizon,
the tall grass is static below
the dark escarpment
of distant thunderstorms
backlit by a still-yellow setting sun.

Nowhere a house, no store.
Only the occasional silo
storing grain or corn,
standing straight and phallic
just past the railroad tracks
that parallel the highway.

And in one day of driving,
the fields embrace
a gently rolling face,
still filled with hay
and wheat or corn,
with oats.

The Eastern Plains: these
are the High Plains of Eastern Colorado,
just before the sighting of mountains
so faint at first they look like clouds,
like white clouds, not black
like the black thunderclouds
of Kansas.

Back in Tennessee, back far in years,
a baby in a tiny table-like bed
with a warmer overhead
like the infrared heaters
keeping French fries hot at McDonald's,
is wheeled into a private room
trailing tubing and ventilator,
for privacy for the parents,
where lights can be turned low,
ambient, not romantic.
The blanket-wrapped baby's body
is handed to the seated parents,
the tube gently un-taped and
solemnly removed,
while tears slip down the parents' cheeks.

And ahead, the vast goldness of wheat
radiates endlessly toward the sun
poised on the horizon's lip.

Holding a Baby

Sometimes things seem
so simple, so certain,
like the still-warm body
of the infant girl
born with the fallible heart
held by her young aunt
when her parents couldn't.

When the aunt asked
"Would you like to hold her?"
–so simple, so certain,
so obvious a choice:
take that body, hold it
like a living infant,
like my own perhaps,
and not like the child
whose heart I couldn't
coax to continue.

Parent Support Group
(Villanelle for a Dead Child)

In a circle they sat, warriors in a wigwam,
tears hidden by lenses and Kleenex
as they told their stories one by one.

Teen sons, cliff-jumping into cold waters,
backseat home-bound sons with dad after hockey.
In a circle they sat, warriors in a wigwam.

A mute girl, wheel-chair bound eight years,
left her father to tell her story to ten strangers,
as they told their stories one by one.

The divorcée decided to become a mother—
fertility clinics, anonymous donor,
as they told their stories one by one.

Two twins came three months early, living on machines,
riding a roller coaster's highs and lows, till one died.
In a circle they sat, warriors in a wigwam,

swapping terrible tales, their children all dead,
no one can understand but the ones in the circle,
as they told their stories one by one.

Despair and deadly pain, they all felt it just the same.
They felt guilty and angry, sometimes suicidal.
In a circle they sat, warriors in a wigwam,
as they told their stories one by one.

Contrition

Iced Tea Poetry

Finality

She hovered weightless above her body still
scintillating slightly, saw the small spot
of blood above the left breast,
and she wondered
how a spot so small
could be so effective,
as the shimmering image
grew blurry and faded into
light and shadow,
and finally into darkness.

Twentieth Anniversary

Waves slap soulfully
at the rocky shore
of Lake Ontario.

A cloud slips under
the sun's crisp disk,
and the trees on the bank
below the grassy knoll
all fall into its shadow,
while the wings of a single duck
stir a commotion of water,
as it lifts airborne,
and disappears, leaving only
the vacuum of solitude.

Twenty-First Anniversary

Dread descends like
humid heat in Memphis July,
like the heartache of absence.

The anniversary comes round
and round, the black horse
on the antique carousel,
the haunting pipe organ caroling.

New Year's Eve

While standing in the dark
on the platform just
feet from the track,
awaiting the raucous rumble
that rolls in without warning,
the platform quakes underfoot.

The cars stilled, the windows glow,
golden nightlights through frosted glass,
and maybe, just maybe,
a face stares out.

The shrill whistle sounds,
the train strains forward,
into the black, its lights
fading in the cold.

I wrap my parka close,
standing again in dark,
on the platform just
feet from the track.

Creation.

Late Night Visitor

When my doorbell rings late at night,
I am startled but I get up from my couch
and limp my way to the front.
I switch on the porch light,
unlock the door and open it
somewhat suspiciously,
only to find no one there.

This happens only rarely,
and it catches me by surprise,
wondering why now, who
is this person ringing
who is not there,

and I close the door,
and I wonder if I am shutting out
someone I wish to see.

Inspiration

Weather is a worthy muse:
gale-strength winds
driving rain horizontal,
lightning spears lighting skies
like the flickering
of a drive-in theater screen.

Or the soft syncopated tap
of gentle raindrops on the metal roof
of a log house in the Colorado Rockies,
seductively trance-inducing
with meandering thoughts
that demand writing down
with an old-fashioned
piston-draw fountain pen,
or a laptop computer screen.

Worthy inspiration is
a partnered couple of geese rising
from near-shore off Lake Ontario.
They ponder a flight south
as season changes, and weather too.

Another: ice on the lake in February,
a meter thick, thick enough
for racing snowmobiles, even tents
with propane fire rings beside a small hole
cut through for ice fishing, or even
the pickerel pulled through that hole,
passing across from its
cold underwater world
through the dark into light,
and then to the frying pan.

Don't look too hard for inspiration,
you'll find it wherever you seek it.

Farewell To Literal Poems

It's been with you since childhood,
so of course it hurts to let it go,
like the timed intervals of labor pains.

Take it in your shaking hand and stroke
and smooth its feathers, feel
its rapid heart beneath your palms,
feel it begin to flutter as you hold it
skyward, and watch as it flies away.

Pens And Indentations

I still have an indentation
in the middle finger of my right hand,
a callous of sorts, but I think more
a bone spur from holding pencils
and then pens many hours a day
for many, many years—
ball points, roller balls,
big broad Sharpies™ before
the discovery of classic fountain pens,
their phallic shapes, the erotic flow
of ink oozing from nib to paper.

That was before the MacIntosh
and the keyboard reinvented it all,
poems once channeled from brain
to pen, to paper in one smooth passage
now filtered, keyboard, computer, screen and printer.

But the finger indentation survives,
and my Mont Blanc still fits,
like a senior man spooning in bed
with his long-suffering senior spouse.

The Importance of a Rabbit

The first truly warm day of spring,
at the edge of a wood deck,
a book of poems in the lap,
there are both the sun's warmth
and a wary gaze—a juvenile rabbit,
a bunny hidden among bee balm stalks
and peonies, foraging cautiously for food.
His gaze shifts nervously,
right and left, wary of dangers.
Looking up from the book,
why is this rabbit so important?

Iced Tea Poetry

A poem is like cold tea.
Once steeped, add ice
and then your own flair—
a splash of lemon juice,
a sprig of mint, perhaps
a raspberry you squeeze
bleeding just before you drop it in.

Then sip its elegance,
and know there will never be
this very same tea again.

ACKNOWLEDGEMENTS

I would like to thank the editors of the following literary journals for featuring certain poems from this collection in their publications, either in their current or an earlier version:

Poetic Hours: Girl in Airport in the Brown Sweater

Door is a Jar Magazine: The Possum; Twentieth Anniversary

Avalon Literary Review: Dexter Loves the Snow

Evening Street Review: Pens and Indentation; Raccoon Hour

Willows Wept Review: Clementines; Ontario Thaw

Muddy River Poetry Review: Mississippi August

Journal of Undiscovered Poets: Sandhill Cranes

California Quarterly: Late Night Visitor

Blood & Thunder: Holding a Baby; My First Seizure

The Blue Mountain Review: KOA

Blueline Magazine: Passing the Amish in Upstate New York; The Birds Know

Intima: A Journal of Narrative Medicine: Doctoring in Nicaragua; New Epileptic; The Lock

Mockingheart Review: Surgery

The Dead Mule School of Southern Literature: Mississippi Delta; Noodling the Wolf River; Cicada Symphony

Dreamers' Creative Writing: Early Blossoms; Ontario Thaw

The Daily Drunk: Getting Dressed After Showering at a KOA Campground

www.ingramcontent.com/pod-product-compliance
Lightning Source LLC
Chambersburg PA
CBHW071358080526
44587CB00017B/3126